Bikes and Bikers

Keith Gaines

Contents

You will meet these abbreviations in this book:

km means kilometres
cc   means cubic centimetres

OXFORD
UNIVERSITY PRESS

The birth of the bike

The first bike was made in 1816. It had no pedals and no brakes. You pushed the ground with your feet to make it go.

It was made of wood. People called it the "hobby horse".

A hobby horse, in a bike race

pedals

Macmillan pedal bike, 1839

In 1839, a Scotsman called Macmillan made the first bike with pedals.

Macmillan was a clever inventor, but he was not very good at riding his bike. In 1842 he ran into a child – he was the first person in the world to be arrested for a bike accident!

People wanted faster bikes. They made the front wheels bigger, so the bikes went further with each turn of the pedals.

In 1882, H. L. Cortis was the first man to cycle more than 20 miles (32 km) in one hour.

H. L. Cortis, 1882

Bikes with one big wheel and one small wheel were called penny-farthings.

The first bike like the ones we
use today was the Rover.
It was made in 1885.

The handlebars steered
the front wheel.

THE ROVER SAFETY BICYCLE (PATENTED).

BRADLEY BIRM.

Safer than any Tricycle, faster and easier than any Bicycle ever made.

A chain from the pedals
turned the back wheel.

Also in 1885, a man called Daimler made an amazing new superbike.

It went faster than any other bike. Instead of pedals it had a motor engine.

A Daimler motorcycle, 1885

twist control to change speed

petrol engine

FACT BOX

Daimler also made motor cars.

In 1901, two brothers called Werner made
a new motorbike.

**The engine was put low
down. This made the bike
less likely to fall over.**

A Werner motorbike, 1901

**The shape of the petrol
tank was fitted into the
bike frame.**

Motorbikes in war

Motorbikes were used in World War I (1914 to 1918). Some bikes were made for special jobs.

This bike had a machine-gun sidecar.

The French Red Cross made motorbike ambulances.

MOTOR CYCLE AMBULANCE

The Golden Age

Many people think the Golden Age of motorbikes was in the 1920s. Some names that were popular in the 1920s are still famous today, such as Harley-Davidson.

Coventry-Eagle

Royal Enfield

Brough Superior

New Imperial

Humber

Harley-Davidson

Triumph

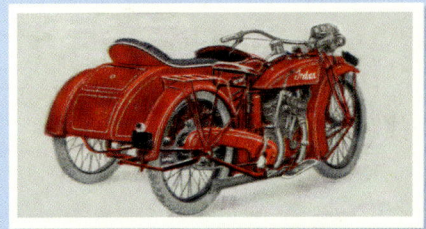

Indian Super-Chief

Mopeds

The first mopeds were pedal bikes with a small motor. You started the motor by pedalling.

Today, few mopeds have pedals, but they all have small engines. Top speed on a moped is 50 km per hour.

A Raleigh moped, 1962

Scooters

The first scooters had smaller engines and smaller wheels than motorbikes. Scooters have running boards to put your feet on.

A Lambretta scooter, 1963

running board

Bikes today

Motorbike or moped?

Some modern mopeds look like motorbikes,
but none of their engines are bigger
than 50cc.

A Gilera H@K, 2000

Motorbike or scooter?

Some modern scooters look more like motorbikes.

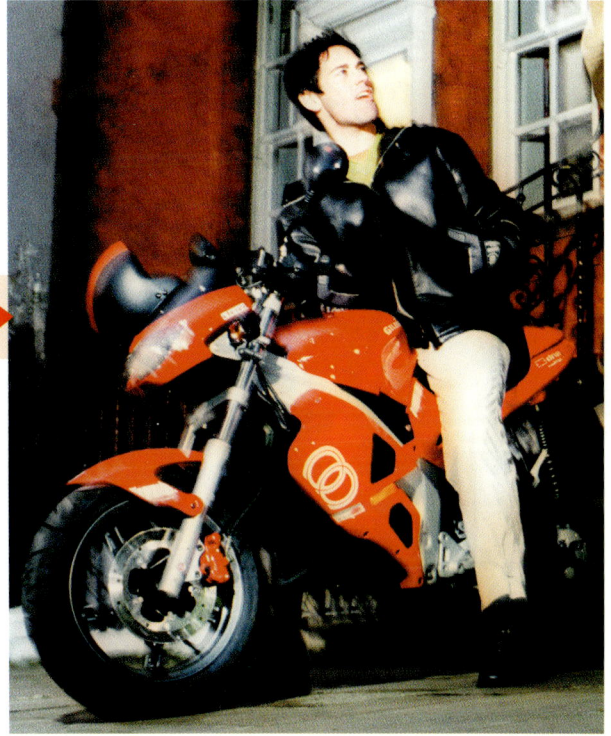

A Gilera DNA

Other modern scooters follow the style of the old scooters.

Some modern scooters, like this Vespa ET4 125, still have running boards.

Bicycles

Chris Boardman rode this ultra-modern pedal bike. It was so high-tech it was banned from some races!

no mudguards

strong frame

thick tyres with deep tread

Cross-country bike racers need tough mountain bikes.

On stunt bikes, you can turn the handlebars and the front wheel all the way round.

Folding bikes are useful in busy cities. They are small, light, and can be folded up to carry on a train.

A unicycle has just one wheel.

A tandem has two or more seats in a line.

A tricycle has three wheels.

A tag-along bike can be fixed to an ordinary bike.

Great bikers

Many bikers have raced into the record books. Here are some of the greatest.

Mike Hailwood

Mike Hailwood won 14 Isle of Man TT (Tourist Trophy) races. His greatest race was in 1965. On the third lap of the TT, he was in the lead. Then he crashed his motorbike, smashing the windscreen and bending the handlebars. He got back on his bike and went on to win.

Mike Hailwood wears the winner's garland at Brands Hatch in 1968.

John Surtees

John Surtees won six TTs and seven world titles. Then he changed from motorbikes to racing cars.

John Surtees on the last lap of a race at Crystal Palace. He did the lap in record time – 1 minute 9.4 seconds.

Barry Sheene

Barry Sheene was as famous for crashing as for winning. He won two World 500 Championships in 1976 and 1977, riding Suzuki motorbikes.

Three serious crashes, which broke many of his bones, cut short his racing career.

Barry Sheen in action, 1980.

Beryl Burton

Beryl Burton won two top British cycling titles,
for Best All-Rounder, and for time trialling
(how far you can ride in a set time).

She won them both for 25 years, every year from 1959 to 1983.

In 1966, she took part in a 12-hour race and covered over 446 km. She beat everyone in the race. As she passed the men's national champion, she offered him a liquorice sweet!

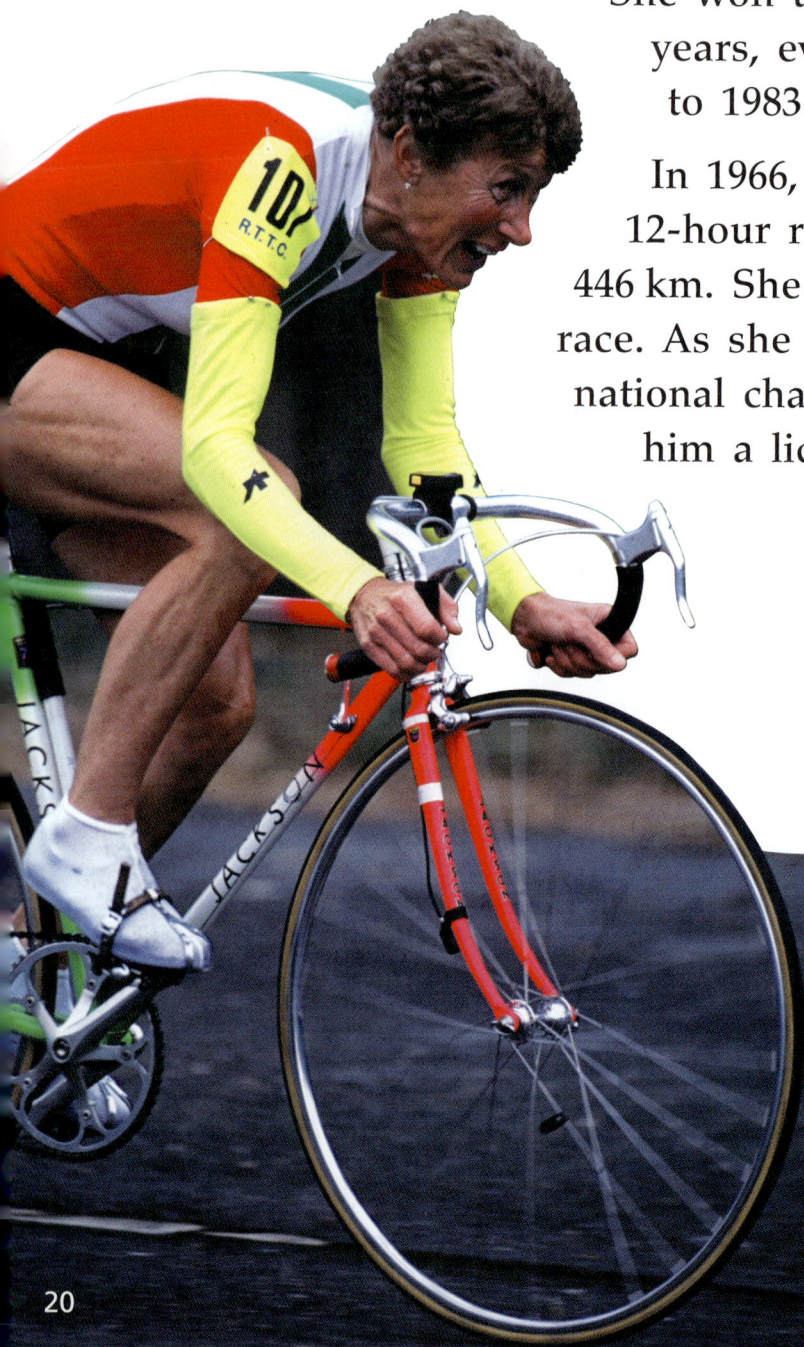

Eddy Merckx

The Tour de France is the toughest cycle race in the world. Eddy Merckx, from Belgium, won the Tour de France five times.

Eddy Merckx wins a world championship race in Switzerland, 1971.

In the Tour de France, cyclists travel 3,500 km, mainly through France. The race lasts 26 days.

Chris Boardman and The Hour record

In 1992, Chris Boardman was the Olympic pursuit champion, but the record he really wanted to break was for "The Hour".

H. L. Cortis was the first man to cycle more than 32 km (20 miles) in one hour (see page 4). Since then the record has been broken many times and the distance covered in one hour has got longer and longer.

Jules Dubois broke The Hour record in 1894.

Some of The Hour record-breakers

Date	Name	Distance
1882	H. L. Cortis	32 km
1894	Jules Dubois	38.22 km
1972	Eddy Merckz	49.43 km

Chris Boardman first broke The Hour record on a very hi-tech bike (see page 14), but this was not allowed as a new record.

In July 1993, his wish finally came true when he rode a normal racing bike for 52.27 km, setting a new world record for The Hour.

Chris Boardman breaking The Hour record in 1993.

Index